a jury of trees

Bilingual Press/Editorial Bilingüe
Canto Cosas

Series Editor
Francisco Aragón

Publisher
Gary Francisco Keller

Executive Editor
Karen S. Van Hooft

Address
Bilingual Press
Hispanic Research Center
Arizona State University
PO Box 875303
Tempe, Arizona 85287-5303
(480) 965-3867

Francisco Aragón
Director of Letras Latinas

Institute for Latino Studies
University of Notre Dame
230 McKenna Hall
Notre Dame, IN 46556
faragon@nd.edu

a jury of trees

poems by

ANDRÉS MONTOYA

edited by

Daniel Chacón

COPUBLISHERS

Bilingual Press/Editorial Bilingüe
TEMPE, ARIZONA

Letras Latinas
NOTRE DAME, INDIANA

Library of Congress Cataloging-in-Publication Data

Names: Montoya, Andrés M., 1968-1999, author. | Chacón, Daniel, editor.
Title: A jury of trees : poems / by Andrés Montoya ; edited by Daniel Chacón.
Description: Tempe, Arizona : Bilingual Press/Editorial Bilingüe ; Notre Dame, Indiana : Letras Latinas, [2016] | Series: Canto Cosas
Identifiers: LCCN 2016032076 | ISBN 9781939743190 (softcover : acid-free paper)
Classification: LCC PS3563.O54588 A6 2016 | DDC 811/.54—dc23
LC record available at https://lccn.loc.gov/2016032076

PRINTED IN THE UNITED STATES OF AMERICA

Front cover art: Andrés Montoya, c. 1998-1999, watercolor. Courtesy of Maceo Montoya
Cover and interior design by John Wincek

Canto Cosas

This poetry series, which was initially supported by awards from the National Endowment for the Arts and the Arizona Commission on the Arts, is designed to give further exposure to Latina and Latino poets who have achieved a significant level of critical recognition through individual chapbooks and publication in periodicals or anthologies or both, but who in most cases have not had their own books of poetry published. Under the watchful eye of series editor, poet, and small press publisher Francisco Aragón, the books in Canto Cosas aim to reflect the aesthetic diversity in American poetry. There are no restrictions on ethnicity, nationality, philosophy, ideology, or language; we will simply continue our commitment to producing high-quality poetry. The books in this series will also feature introductions by more established voices in the field.

oración

i do not want
to lose your mouth
—open and wet
like a yellow leaf—
here,
my eyes are for you

carry them like seeds
in your pocket.

i walk but
i do not always understand
the rhythm of street signs.

fill me with your breath
a kiss that teaches song
to the little boy
on the curb.

CONTENTS

II

III

IV

leukemia poems

ACKNOWLEDGEMENTS

This collection took years to put together, as many of the poems were scattered on stray, handwritten scraps of paper, floppy disks, and in the pages of personal journals.

I could not have done this alone. I'd like to thank Andrés's family, Lezlie Salkowitz-Montoya, Malaquías Montoya, Maceo Montoya, and JoAnna Kerby. I'd also like to thank Francisco Aragón, who made this possible, and Lee Herrick, Michael Medrano, Tim Z. Hernández, Juan Felipe Herrera, Laurie Ann Guerrero, Corrinne Clegg Hales, and the late Philip Levine.

Thank you to all who helped me with transcribing and deciphering, including some brilliant students in the MFA program at UTEP, Silvana Ayala, Lau Cesarco, Daniela Gónzalez Armijo, Carlos Espinoza, and Blake Nemic. I know I'm leaving people out —I'm so sorry, it took a really long time and memory fades—but my love for everyone who has ever been touched by Montoya's poetry is powerful, and I am filled with gratitude. Thank you, thank you, thank you.

FOREWORD

Portrait of the Chicano Artist as a Pot-Smoking, Young Christian Man

Daniel Chacón
THE UNIVERSITY OF TEXAS AT EL PASO

Andrés Montoya is dead. There is no need to mourn his short life; what's done is done, the dead are dead, let them bury their own. Does that sound insensitive? This is something he strongly believed when he was living, that you mourn the dead at the moment of their death, but then you move on, back into the world of the living, because when the body dies the spirit soars to unbelievable heights, a freedom the living can never understand. People were stunned by how bravely he faced death. They were unhappier than he was, cried more than he did. They frowned with dark faces while his face glowed with light, because fundamental to his beliefs was that death is a new beginning, that he would not suffer in the afterlife, whereas the rest of us had to stick around and suffer this world. For those of us he left behind, it would be better for us to help and love those who are still alive than to hang onto our image of the dead one. Definitely, there shall be no communication with the dead, even about such small questions to them as, *What would you have wanted?* He agreed with Wislawa Szymborska when she wrote, "*The dead don't know any more than we do.*"

Whatever meaning we give to the life of a dead person is filtered through our own needs and desires. We give ultimate meaning to them because they are not here to give meaning to their own lives. Therefore, I will not be so arrogant as to say this collection of poetry, this second Andrés Montoya book of poems, this very first of his posthumous books, is exactly how he would have put it together. I won't say, *He would have wanted it this way.*

How would I know such a thing? The last time I had a conversation with him was in his hospital bed, about a week before he died, as he was writing in his journal, "leukemia poems," some of which appear in part three of this book. He had peace on his face and light in his eyes.

Besides, do we really care what the dead want? If we do we need to quit reading the works of Kafka, the ones that remained unpublished during his lifetime, that is, almost everything he wrote, including every one of his novels. His dying wish to his best friend, Max Broad, was to burn everything, destroy every word he had ever written, to never let us read *The Castle, The Trial,* and a novel he never finished about the United States, which we know today as the brilliant book *Amerika.* Are we not happy that his best friend denied his dying wish? Many critics believe, among them Jorge Luis Borges, that Kafka didn't really want Max to burn all of his manuscripts. If that was what he really wanted, asks Borges, why didn't he do it himself? It's not that he was on his deathbed when he made the request. He was still healthy, looking into the future. But even if Kafka wasn't lying and he really wanted his manuscripts to be burnt, aren't we glad his best friend didn't pay attention to him? Aren't we glad that he ignored his dying wishes? Kafka belongs to us now, to our common literary heritage, not to the body that used to house his stunning creative soul.

Still, before Andrés Montoya died of leukemia, when he knew he was dying, he pulled me aside, saying he had something he needed to speak to me about. He didn't literally "pull me aside," because he was in his hospital bed, the bed he would die in, and he couldn't move around much. He couldn't take me out to the hallways, and we couldn't do one of his favorite activities, walking through the city with no destination, *sin rumbo*, just talking about anything, mostly about God and poetry and the plight of the people, our people, Chicano/as and the poor.

On his hospital bed, he pulled me aside with a gesture, which told the others in the room that he needed to speak to me. One by one they drifted into the hallways of the hospital, and I waited by his bed, wondering what my dying friend wanted.

At this time in his life, when he was dying in the hospital, people always visited him, so many people surrounding his bed, having what we all feared would be our last conversation before he died—Steve Yarborough, Corrinne Clegg Hales, Philip Levine, Gary Soto, all the talented members of the Montoya family.

Everyone came to comfort him, but he was so convinced in his faith and so full of love that he ended up comforting *them*, ministering to *them*, holding *their* hands and assuring them that everything would be all right. He even prayed with some people who had forgotten how to pray.

But this time when he pulled me aside, I knew he wanted to talk about himself. When everyone left the room, he told me he knew he was going to die, and after he did, he wanted me to take over his poetry, by which he meant, he explained, he wanted to turn it over to me, all of it, and I should decide what to do with it.

He didn't tell me what he wanted me to do with his life's work. He didn't say publish this first, then this, then that. He didn't say which journals he wanted me to send out to, which publishers he wanted me to seek, he just told me he wanted me to take over his poetry. It's all on his computer, he said, his Mac Classic, and the rest in notebooks he had been keeping for years, including his MFA thesis.

Do what you think is best.

I had known Andrés since he was 18 years old, and we were roommates for many years, both of us students at Fresno State. We lived in the Meadow Woods, across from the university, which people referred to back then as the Ghetto Woods, before the buildings became re-gentrified. There were a lot of gang bangers living there, a lot of fighting, a lot of drugs. I remember one time Andrés and I were on the balcony, which had a view of the pool, and some white guy right out of prison—who half an hour earlier had yelled up to our balcony asking if we wanted to buy some hash—was now talking to some hard-looking white boys. Quicker than we could stand up, they beat him and he was floating in the pool with blood coming out of his ear, and the boys ran away between the buildings of the apartment complex. I could tell a gaggle of stories about that place, the gunshots, the drug deals below our windows, the crazy redheaded man who would walk around the complex shirtless in the wee hours of the dark morning, yelling, *I want to fuck!*

Let's just say it earned its nickname, and it was where we lived as roommates for five years, where we came into language.

Although Andrés had wanted to write poetry all of his life, we pretty much became writers in the Ghetto Woods. I was trying to graduate with a degree in Political Science, a bachelor's I had been working on for ten years, working restaurant jobs full time some semesters, so involved with Chicano activism other semesters. I was finally going to be granted a degree in one semester, after which I had planned on going to law school. I decided that since I had to go to school anyway, I would take a Creative Writing class with Corrinne Clegg Hales.

It changed my life. I would sit in our apartment across the street from Fresno State with both my windows open, breeze coming into the room, and I would write on my little Brother word processor all night long, writing, writing, writing.

Whenever I would finish a story, or think that the story was finished, I would yell for Andrés, because I wanted to read it to him. He would sit on my bed as I sat in the chair before my desk reading aloud what I had just written, and he would be awed. He was the best audience a new Chicano writer could ask for because he saw the brilliance in everything.

He gave me the confidence I needed to continue to make the decision to give up everything else to be a writer, to give up the notion of ever being a lawyer.

Sometimes I had to bribe him to come into my room and listen to my work. Other times I would have to follow him from room to room as I read, and sometimes, just to piss me off or if he wasn't in a good mood, he would shake his head before I even finished and say, "That's a bunch of shit. Try again, mi'jo."

Sometimes I would bribe him with pot. I had a pretty good connection at the time, when most of Fresno and our friends were dry, so I always had good pot. Whenever I was about to light up, I would yell *Sparkee!*

I yelled as loud as I could, *Sparkee!*

If Andrés responded with a primordial *Ugh!* that meant he wanted to join me, and I would wait with my manuscript for him to get there. It was the price of smoking my weed.

Writing is contagious. My obsession filled the apartment and he breathed it in, and after a while in that apartment, all night long I would be in my bedroom typing away, writing, writing, writing, and he would be in the next room typing on his Mac Classic, a gift from his father, but instead of writing history papers, he would be writing poem after poem after poem. When he was finished with something he thought was particularly brilliant, which was every other poem, or whenever I had a piece of fiction that I thought would change the world, which was every other piece, we would seek each other out and read to each other.

Andrés was the very first Chicano student body president at Fresno State, or I should say "radical Chicano" president. I was a senator representing the school of Social Sciences, both of us active in protests, meetings, anti-Columbus day celebrations. Naturally, when we became obsessed with writing, and when Andrés—a history major with plans to go on to earn a PhD (he saw himself as a leftist professor at some university)—announced to me that all he really wanted was to write poetry, we took our activism into literature.

With a couple of other Chicano students, Teresa Navarro, Víctor Canales, and Markanthony Alvídrez, we started the Chicano Writers and Artists Association (CWAA) and we invited Chicano/a poets to campus, the first being one of our local heroes, Omar Salinas, the Crazy Gypsy himself. We also organized what we called guerrilla readings, where a bunch of us Chicano students—poets pounding with passion—would invade and occupy an area of campus, the free speech area, the entrance to the bookstore, the Quad where all the Chicano/a students hung out, and we read our poetry aloud. We started a literary journal called *Pachuco Children Hurl Stones,* which was a line from an Omar Salinas poem, a journal that still exists today at Fresno State. Meanwhile, Montoya was learning so much about the craft in the workshops of Philip Levine and Peter Everwine that he was getting good fast.

Of course, back then we had no idea that Montoya would soon be dead, that he would find out he had leukemia right after his first book won the UC Irvine Chicano/Latino Literary Prize. He would die before it came out, but he got to see the cover, and he liked it. He would never hold it or know that it would go on to win the American Book Award. All we knew at the time was that our lives had become dedicated to the word.

And we worked, creating a writer's workshop out of our living room where other Chicano/a writers would come by to read their stuff. We had impromptu poetry readings on the balcony as if all the Ghetto Woods would stop and hear what we had to say.

With each other, we became very honest in the critiques of our work, and as he studied with Levine and read many poets and poetic theory, his understanding of the craft amazed me, and his poetry grew. At first, when he first started writing poems, his work was full of passion and commitment to the Chicano movement, and women, and God. That was the holy trinity of his early work. And a lot of it, quite frankly, wasn't that great.

I remember one time he was very excited about a poem that he had just written. "You got listen to this, man!" he said. "I think this is one of my best!"

I sat on the couch and he stood before me. He was a big guy. He always wore a prison jacket, baggy Ben Davis work pants, and black work boots. He had long hair in a ponytail.

He stood before me, his body filling the room.

Suddenly he blurted out, loud as thunder, *"Democracy! Ha!"*

That was the title of the poem.

"You call this democracy?" he screamed.

Ha!
This isn't a democracy!
This is oppression!

It was the worst poem ever written.

For years to come I would tease him about it, and it became a metaphor to us, so whenever we would encounter a naïve but passionate poem written by one of our students, we would call it a "Ha! Democracy!" poem.

His early poems were often didactic, cliché, full of passion, but some of them were damn good, and he got better and better. He loved to write, and he loved to read, to discover new poets, but at first the Latin American poet he knew best was Roque Dalton, whose poems he used to read aloud and then blurt out, "Isn't that brilliant!"

He kept discovering more poets.

I remember when he came home with a new book and said, "You got to hear this," and he proceeded to read Li Young Lee's "The City in Which I Love You." He was awed by it, and he caused me to see the brilliance in the poem. That was one of his gifts, he knew how to spot the brilliance, not only in poetry, but in every child of God. He knew how to see Christ in the brown eyes of a child.

He loved poetry. He would stop and re-read a line, picture it, feel it with his eyes closed and then say, "Isn't that brilliant?"

And he grew and grew and grew, and with strong letters of recommendation from Philip Levine and Corrinne Clegg Hales he was accepted into the University of Oregon's MFA, a program that only accepted six poets a year out of over three hundred applications. He left Fresno for the first time in years and went to study under Garrett Hongo and TR Hummer.

I had also applied to the MFA at the University of Oregon the exact same year, so when Montoya was accepted, we were certain I wouldn't be. We figured he would be their Chicano quota, that they wouldn't need another one of us, wouldn't want another one of us, but then one day I too got the call from Garret Hongo welcoming me into the program.

We were very suspicious, both of us being Chicano activists. Two Chicanos accepted into the same program that only accepted twelve a year, six poets and six fiction writers? Hmmm.

We thought for sure the FBI had a hand in it, that they wanted us together so we could be closely monitored. Of course, we overestimated our political efficacy and ultimately we were both happy to have been accepted; now, in retrospect, I know the FBI had nothing to do with it. I believe that if there were a force that kept us together for another two years where we grew even more as writers, where we read so many good books and wrote constantly for two years and continued our discussions about poetics, politics, and religion, where we even had the opportunity to teach poetry and fiction to brilliant undergraduate white students, it was Grace. It was the hand of God, the motion of the universe, the serendipity of fate, whatever language one wants to use.

So we went from being roommates in Fresno to roommates in Eugene, Oregon, and it was during those two years Andrés's life changed forever.

Let's call it the conversion.

It happened during the summer, when he earned wages digging ditches. I kid you not, he dug ditches during the summer. Although everyone who got accepted into the program was granted a TAship, we were pretty much on our own during the summer, and unlike many of the other students, we couldn't go to Europe or back to the East Coast for the summer and live in our parents' summer home, nor could we afford to stay in Eugene without pay. We couldn't afford to go back to Fresno either, because we had no jobs there. Besides, we couldn't afford to move our stuff or pay rent while we weren't occupying a place in Eugene, so we had to find jobs. I was fortunate enough to get a job teaching with the Creative Writing Department, but Andrés had to look through the want ads, and he found a job digging ditches. He would leave early in the morning and come back late afternoon, his clothes full of mud and his face smeared with dirt like a black-and-white photograph of a coal miner. When he got home he was so tired all he wanted to do was sleep. During the evenings he would lie on the floor in the living room, which served as his bedroom, and he read the Bible. He had always been a Christian, ever since I knew him, but he'd been a radical Chicano Christian, a chain-smoking, beer-drinking Christian, a Christian who smoked pot and cussed like a Mexican truck driver. But something happened that summer. He didn't want to go out and drink beer or go listen to music or smoke pot and walk around the city. He didn't want to drop acid, like we had done many times before in Fresno, or go to parties. All he wanted to do was stay home and read the Bible. He would pray all the time, and he would weep as he thought about the life he had led.

"I've done some messed up things in my life," he would tell me.

He quit smoking, cold turkey, a man who used to smoke more than a pack a day, and whenever I was in my bedroom, where I would be writing another story that I thought would change the world, and I yelled *Sparkee!*, he didn't return the primordial *Ugh!*

It was at this time that his poetry began to change as well. It was at this time that he started reading the Latin American greats, Pablo Neruda, César Vallejo, Octavio Paz. For many years he had been reading the North American poets, learning North American poetic tradition, or as he used to call it, cracker craft.

Now if he wasn't reading his Bible, he was reading poetry and essays about poetry, and he questioned what they were teaching him in class. He read Lorna Dee Cervantes and marveled at her political commitment and her beautiful craft. One of his favorite poems was "Poem to the White Man Who Wonders How I, an Intelligent Well-Read Woman, Can Believe in the War of the Races," and he read aloud over and over again the line, "Sharp-shooting goose-steppers round every corner."

"Isn't that brilliant?"

He evokes that line in "pákatelas," the final poem in *whispered fruit,* the posthumous manuscript included in this collection. In that poem, published in its entirety by *in the grove,* he writes about how he developed as a poet and how he soon learned that North American poetry asserts its own superiority, how Chicano writers are ignored, their traditions discounted, like those rooted in Nezahualcoyotl, the Mexican indigenous poet king.

For many years Montoya lived with his mom and his sister across the street from Radio Park, on the poor side of Fresno, a park where at night there were crack dealers and all kinds of crazy things going on. Notice how much he refers to Radio Park in his poetry, not just this book, but his first one, too. It was for him a symbol of the barrio, and he found it ironic that Radio Park was where the Fresno Museum of Art was located. This was where the Fresno Poets Association had big readings, with the biggest poets from all over the country. Everyone knows about the Fresno poets, how Philip Levine brought so much poetry to Fresno and changed its literary landscape. Much of it took place at the Fresno Museum of Art, in Radio Park.

He criticizes the poetic culture, but at the same time he honors the poetry and poets. Whereas the "academy" might turn dead white men into idols to be worshipped and used as a means of cultural oppression, he could still find the brilliance in their works. He loved Walt Whitman, Shakespeare, William Carlos Williams, or rather, he loved their words. As I said, Montoya was a big guy, and he had a running joke about his size. He would indicate his own stature and say, "I'm large. I contain multitudes."

The collection *whispered fruit* was written after he received his MFA at the University of Oregon, after his first book was accepted for publication, but before he knew he was dying. It was after the conversion, after the repentance, and it is a book about coming into language, about finding his poetic voice, or rather the poetic tradition to which he belongs.

I remember one day he came home from a poetry workshop at the University of Oregon, angry, slamming down his book bag, and saying "Those gabachos don't know anything. Do you know that they say you shouldn't use the word *soul* or *love?*! What is wrong with those people? Neruda uses them all the time. Cracker craft!"

In "pákatelas" he writes,

> i speak words forbidden:
> hope love
> beauty faith
> soul spirit.

He didn't care if he was discouraged in workshops from using such heavy-handed words. He used them anyway.

And what does *pákatelas* mean?

For him, in his ear, it was the sound of working in a packing house, packing peaches or tomatoes or whatever was in season, the foremen looking over your shoulder, yelling in your ear, "Pack those things!" in a valley Spanglish, "¡pákatelas!"

It is the rhythm of work.

¡Pákatelas! ¡Pákatelas!

It was the music of the poor. His heritage was just as much from the Spanish language poets as it was from the North American poets that he admired so much. He began to read Lorca, Darío, Gabriela Mistral. He had been told so often in his workshops that he shouldn't write political poetry that he was happy to discover that in Latin America political poetry abounds.

And all the while he was reading the Bible, and he came to a point in his life where he didn't want to be a poet as much as he wanted to be a good Christian, as much as he wanted to save souls. People who knew him while he was dying knew of his evangelical fervor. And he was sincere about it. He wasn't a hypocritical Christian who did one thing and preached another. He was committed to Christ. If you look closely at his first book, *the ice worker sings and other poems,* you will see the evangelical nuances. Most of those poems were written before the conversion, edited afterwards, but many of them, including the letters, were written after that summer in Eugene, and they carry messages for his friends and family about salvation through Christ.

The book contract came after the conversion, and I remember he changed a lot of the "F" words to more mild exclamations. For example, in the poem "locura," he had originally written "this fucked up thing called life," but after the conversion he changed it to "this crazy cosa called life," which might sound better anyway. Some of the poems that he wrote before the conversion he didn't even want to include in the manuscript, because they were too worldly.

He wasn't a new Andrés. He was the same guy, but his priorities were different.

Still, he was a poet, and *whispered fruit* is all about being a poet. It's not about salvation, although within it you will find the grace of God. It's not about Jesus Christ, although his footsteps are all over the pages; it's about being a poet. It's about the word.

 have included poems from both before and after the conversion, and from before leukemia and after he got the word that he was dying.

The first section of this manuscript, "colón-ization," includes poems he wrote when he was still a radical Chicano poet, going to protests and putting his face into the face of his opponents and calling them racists. Like a lot of California Chicanos, Andrés wasn't fluent in Spanish, but he was around it all his life and used words here and there when he spoke. The first time he heard Christopher Columbus referred to by a Chicano poet as *Colón* he thought it was a joke, that the poet was calling Columbus an asshole, a colon. He didn't know that was how you say Columbus in Spanish. He showed me the poem and said, "Check it out! Colón. Pinche Colón!"

So when he put together this early collection and called it "colón-ization" he was essentially making a statement about how imperialism created a culture of assholes, like the asshole-ization of the Americas. In this section he uses a few expletives, which I've kept in their original form.

Montoya was very influential on young Chicano poets, and I think one of the reasons, other than his beautiful language, was his commitment to the movement and to the people, to crying out for justice. In these poems he does that. Some of them were part of his MFA thesis at the University of Oregon, and others were poems he wrote his first year at Oregon. A poem he worked on for many years is "lorena's whisper." He wrote the first draft when we were in our apartment in the Ghetto Woods. He would read it to me, draft after draft, and it was a poem that really mattered to him. I remember the tears coming to his eyes.

Even if at the moment of his death this poem didn't matter to him, it mattered a lot during his lifetime. I also included a poem about his friend Prax. You'll see that this name comes up a lot in his poetry, not only in "colón-ization" but in *whispered fruit* and his first book. This is the story of Prax. I know it mattered to him.

Would he have wanted me to include these early poems? They are, after all, not very evangelical. They do not avoid cuss words. Some of them are even sexually charged.

I don't know what he wanted when he said, "Take over my poetry," but I know that he didn't tell me what he wanted. How easy that would have been for him to do. He could've said, "Take out all the poems that don't reflect my Christianity, that are not about my love for Christ," but he said no such thing.

He could've asked some of his more mature Christian friends to take over his poetry. Many of them knew poetry and used to write with him and do workshops with him. He could've asked them, knowing that they would suppress those poems that did not represent the Gospel, but he didn't ask them. He asked me.

We would talk on the phone for hours, or walk through the city for hours, talking about God, talking about my life, about his life, so he knew where I was, spiritually speaking. He prayed for me all the time. He wanted me to find the light. No, he didn't ask me to take over his poetry because I was a good Christian.

I think he wanted me to handle the poetry because I knew him as a poet. I was there from the beginning. I was there at the end. I knew not only what the dying Montoya wanted, but I knew what he would have wanted at 19, and what he would've wanted at 21, and 24, 25, 26, 27, 28, and so on until he died at 31, because I was there the entire time watching his poetry grow, watching his spiritual passion glow. What he wanted at one point of his life when I knew him would change over the years, evolve as it were, or "become," like we "become" over a lifetime. What he would have wanted once dead, when his spirit left this body, what perspective he would have on the meaning of his life, I have no idea. He's dead. I cannot ask him.

But I know that no one is just the person they are at the moment of his or her death. He or she is the person created over a lifetime, as filtered through and understood by the rest of us. All of his life, Montoya never quit caring about the word, and the manuscript I included in this volume, *whispered fruit,* shows that love for language. I like to think he would've wanted that manuscript to be represented exactly as it is. It was, after all, the only complete posthumous manuscript.

But his love for poetry also shows in his early work, and he never quit caring about the Chicano experience. He never forgot where he came from. He never stopped writing about Fowler and Fresno and Radio Park.

Before he sent *the ice worker sings* to the Chicano Literary Contest, he asked me to go over it, and I did. I edited it. I made suggestions about line breaks and word choices, most of which he took, some of which he didn't.

I have also included some poems never seen by anyone, right out of his journal while dying in the hospital, when he knew he had but a few weeks/days left. He, not me, called them "leukemia poems." These poems are simply fragments, images and thoughts of death. During the last days, he would pick up his journal, write in it in pencil, and he drew pictures too. None of the poems are complete in the conventional sense.

For me, putting together this section of the book was the most difficult, even though what he felt shows incredible courage and faith. What would you write if you were certain death awaited days away? These poems are beautiful, and as tough as it was to go through them, this book would not be complete without them. They are often prayer-like. Some of them rise to the level of Rumi. He writes, "One day God fell in love." It's a poem about love, not death, but the joy of love, which never left him.

The final fragment in this section is, I believe, the last words he wrote, because after this, I cannot find anything.

His very last written words include

Something behind my eyes
wants to leap
into this evening

This evokes some of the more mystical poems of Li Young Lee from his most mature book, *Behind My Eyes,* a book that would not come out until years after Montoya's death. It shows that Montoya, moments from dying, got a glimpse into the beyond, saw beyond the veil, which is the source of great poetry, the common heritage of all artists. These "leukemia poems" are the words of a brave poet, a warrior who had no choice but to conquer fear of death. They are a testament to his faith.

I think he knew that I would care about the poetry, and I think that's why he asked me to take over his work. He wanted me to present his poetry, so here it is, some of the poems Andrés Montoya left behind in that Mac Classic and in notebooks.

With one published book and with one life dedicated to social justice and spiritual development, Andrés changed the direction of Chican@ poetry. His name was not only given to the most important Latino poetry prize in the nation, responsible for publishing the first books of such poets as Sheryl Luna, Paul Martínez Pompa, Emma Telles, Laurie Ann Guerrero, and David Campos, but his poetry also influenced such brilliant young writers as Tim Z. Hernández, Michael Medrano, Marisol Baca, Lee Herrick, and his own little brother Maceo Montoya, whose first novel, *The Scoundrel and the Optimist,* came out in 2010. In Chicano literature, *the ice worker sings* has become a classic.

I don't care much to opine about whether at the moment of his death, if I were able to hand him a copy of *a jury of trees,* he would approve of it exactly the way it's published here, but I know that I love the poetry within these pages.

It represents the poet not only at the very moment of his death, but also in his youth. I like to believe that the twenty-year-old Andrés Montoya, who stood over me like a giant and read "Ha! Democracy!" as if he was reading King Lear (*Blow winds! Crack your cheeks!*), would be thrilled to see these poems, would be thrilled that he wrote them. I like to believe that the dying Andrés Montoya, who asked me a favor, would love to see *whispered fruit* published in its entirety. All these poems, the early ones and the posthumous ones, are beautiful not only for their language and precociousness and masterful sense of craft, but because of their strong political assertion. This book shows his development as an artist and a spiritual being. It is Montoya's second book, and like a lot of second books, it's his *Portrait* book, that is, his *Portrait of a Chicano Artist as a Young Man.* It's his story the way he wrote it.

His capacity to see brilliance everywhere made him a brilliant poet, and one of the most loving human beings I have ever had the privilege to learn from. I do not mourn his death here, but oh how I mourn his death. Still, I am grateful he left some words behind, that his soul can speak for itself.

INTRODUCTION

Dying Softly to His Song: Poetics of Love and Dissolution in Andrés Montoya's *a jury of trees*

Stephanie Fetta
SYRACUSE UNIVERSITY

Written over a fifteen-year period, the poems of *a jury of trees* may seem disparate. The first group of poems, "colón-ization," written in the ripening blush of adulthood, are full of the vigor of a healthy mind, voice, and body, much like the second group, *whispered fruit*, a manuscript completed before Montoya learned he was terminally ill. By the third group, however, the "leukemia poems," Andrés lay dying in a hospital room, preparing for his full communion with life through death. Over the course of the poems that comprise this volume, Montoya's lived experience changes radically, yet the poems form a collection through his fidelity to two philosophical premises: the universal, nonhierarchical subjectivity of the animate and inanimate, and life as the unrelenting experience of humility. The striking poetics of Andrés Montoya could be illustrated in numerous poems; however, I point the reader to "generation" as an early moment in the collection when these forces coalesce, providing form and frame to *a jury of trees* as a whole. This poem stands out as an example of Montoya's exquisite use of language, presenting a democratized sense of self and the world, where, through the humility of stutters and the inspiration of whispers, the poetic voice dies softly to his song.

A long poem comprising part I of *whispered fruit*, "generation" begins on a forsaken night as the speaker traces the collective woes of his barrio through the voice of his sister, who, sequestered in a public latrine, sobs the name of God. The poetic I enters the poem omnisciently with the ability to observe the cosmic forces at work in the urban decay of the street corner, the drug-induced enthusiasm of a woman's holler over a public phone, sirens blaring in a sonic everywhere. The final wails of despair, we might conclude, presuppose their futility. These cries do not seem to appeal to God but rather vocalize a God *not* present, one who will *not* listen, who will leave such pleas unanswered. The poetic I parses a cry of foregone hope into a stutter, a disfluent, *striving-towards* enunciation. This scene of hell on earth is found in Montoya's descriptions of architecture, space, objects, and sounds, in the relationship of the State to the Latin@/x underclass, and in the demeaning ways we often treat others and ourselves. But these same manifestations of hate and despair equally express the divine forces on a continuum with the starry sky, the warm sun, a bruised peach, and riotous cockroaches.

Narrating the weeping of the poetic I's sister, section 6 of this poem graphs her location in a city block where ambient sounds and visual unrest heighten the poet's awareness that "something's going on," a line twice repeated in separate stanzas. Geography becomes a living entity in this poem, a force unto itself troped throughout the collection, where, in near cinematographic fashion, the poetic voice moves indoors from the bus stop where his sister has been waiting in grief-stricken unease, a hell "doing an imitation / of a street corner" (12-13), to find sanctuary in a public bathroom stall where she exclaims, "God! God!" (24).

The divine drama unveiled in the quotidian despair of late capitalist underclass America comes "like a stutter" (26), a bodily expression, a corporeal prayer initiating Montoya's spiritual search as a whole.

> i stutter.
> this is not like singing.
> this is like penance. (section 7, "generation," 1-3)

Whereas the stutter cues spiritual yearning, the whisper connects poetic subjects to the divine. This second aural category carefully attends to the whirling sound of the wind, the beat of the swaying trees, as messages coextensive with Christ's breath, a physical whisper of his presence into and onto the I's perception as evidenced in section 2 of "generation":

> i watch
> young lovers
> . . . .
> they breathe
> like the trees
> praising God.

In contrast to involuntary autonomic breathing, Montoya's whispered breath is a sounded, intentional conveyance, the force of which is found again in section 8 of "generation," where the I implores:

> *breathe, o God*
>   *o Christ*
>
> *breathe your tree's fruit*
>   *red, riverlike* (26-29)

This whisper, the same kind that instructs him and his sister "to sing" in the later poem "song lesson," first comes to his sister as a stutter (section 6, "generation," 26), an initial embodied will that, in its brokenness, admits the possibility of change.[1] Although breath figures in many biblical verses signaling life and the presence of God, the sister (like the grandmother and the female lovers in Montoya's other poems) is the agent of the Christian message—the feminine divine authority working God's message through suffering humanity.

Stuttering, then, finds the divine in whispers and eventually forms into song, a poetic performative invoking the Chican@/x tradition of *flor y canto*, the Aztec practice of singing poetry, which became a preferred mode of expression during the Chicano movement of the 1960-70s.[2] Montoya inscribes his poetry in the genealogy of *flor y canto* by frequently using the words "singing" and "song," which, within his teleology, signal spiritual completion in the performative of writing and then reading his poetry. Shifting from stutter to whisper to song suggests an embodied process that seeks to stimulate a simultaneity of times, spaces, and subjects, a way of living in death and dying to life.

Further, invoking *flor y canto* trifurcates the colonial histories of Spanish subjugation of indigenous America, English colonialism of North America, and US colonialism of Mexican and Chican@/x populations since the 1848 Treaty of Guadalupe Hidalgo, which officially ended the US-Mexican War but was ineffective in ending colonizing practices against Mexicans and their descendants. The poem comprising part IV of *whispered fruit*, "pákatelas," combines stuttering, breathing, and singing within these colonial histories and spiritual salvation:

> my throat vibrates
>   from boats
>   and land.
>   sometimes i
>   sing

with my spanish
eyebrow.

but always
my tewa nostrils
demand to know
the meaning of song
and flor
y
canto.
(section 2, 13-26)

Though the historic and actual social tensions affect the speaker down to his eyebrow, colonizing—a damaging social practice—nevertheless cannot stultify his experience of global subjectivity, a fluidity of perspectives Montoya renders in personified toes, trees, cockroaches, and sky. In other instances, even a bench, a street corner, and a peach are treated as sensate objects.

This fluidity recalibrates relations between all things in our world, situating the speaker who, like us, is relativized as one point and type of life among fields of life. This collection closes with the prayerlike "leukemia poems," written while Montoya lay close to death, in which he maintains the same interests and concerns expressed in the two philosophical premises highlighted in "generation."[3] Condensed in scope, the "leukemia poems" are similar to haiku. All untitled, they feature an imagistic brevity that is especially appreciable the more familiar the reader is with Montoya's work. In the antepenultimate poem, Montoya writes:

one day i asked God to stamp eternity on my eyes.
i didn't know what i was saying. i only knew that i
wanted to understand cheekbones and the hope of
clouds. (1-4)

In Montoya's etiology, we read of the desire to experience divine presence, to feel the poetic self in communion with God, to physically receive the marks of salvation on the speaker's body.

Consider this in relation to his earlier poems such as "face" (part III, *whispered fruit*), where the speaker is:

> . . . waiting
> to understand
> the poverty
> of your cheek. (1-4)

And again, in "pákatelas" the speaker states:

> i wanted to understand the madness
>   of my own divided
>
>   cheeks. (section 2, 242-44)

We can recognize cheeks as facial features whose expressiveness is sometimes more powerful and authentic than one's own eyes. Throughout the volume, the speaker wants to understand how life inhabits disparate parts of the self, largely outside of the control and intention of the mind.[4] Likewise, recognizing clouds as hopeful illustrates the composite environment of the subjective forces that the speaker inhabits. Geographically, he is earthbound; the clouds he remarks upon are far off but nevertheless a spiritual presence. Personification is a strong aesthetic in Montoya's poetry, and in particular, clouds, like stars, are not only markers of the upward motion of salvation common in Judeo-Christian cosmology, but they themselves are full of life, their hope, agential and influential, coding their environs laterally and horizontally with feelings and intentions.

Clearly influenced by Federico García Lorca, Walt Whitman, Pablo Neruda, and Luis Omar Salinas, Montoya's poetry also bears similarities to the poetry of Mary Oliver, Czelaw Milosz, Wallace Stevens, and Nazim Hikmet. Montoya sees life in the small, the inert, everyday violence and grief, the seemingly unimportant, and the local until his vision sweeps upward and outward to the sky, the moon, and the stars. He creates his divine etiology literally from the ground up, often introducing the poetic I later in his poems, already poetically and divinely defined within and among the laughing cockroaches in the poem "cucarachas" (in "colón-ization"), and the wailing ants in section 3 of "generation." Even a peach, emblematic of the agribusiness and canning industry of the Fresno region, opens to join the speaker in the second untitled leukemia poem so that "together we'll be a song" (3), proclaiming the peach's ". . . breath / soft and orange / like a child dancing" (9-11).

A symphony of forces deftly expresses the divinity embodied in each, regardless of the merit of their individual behavior. Such is the case in "generation," from whence the collection's title is taken. In section 7 of the poem, the speaker proposes his religious devotion to "a jury of trees," a terrestrial delegation of God's will materially evident in their upright stature, their longevity, and their silent and imposing strength. He further elucidates in his poem "declaration" in part II of *whispered fruit:*

> i will look for truth
> in the rough skin
> of wood (14-16)

The texture of bark in the poem "song lesson," as tactilely and emotionally communicative as a human hand, attributes to the tree a human form, capable of intimacy:

> the glare of the trees' red bark
> demanding my hand,
> skin upon skin (part II, *whispered* fruit, 6-8)

In an eponymous poem, Montoya poetically renders the tree a central actor in the Christ drama. In "tree" the I ponders the intention, role, experience, and purpose of a common tree, thus emblematizing trees across time and space such that this tree in a Fresno park becomes the speaker's interlocutor and the tree hewn for the crucifixion a sacred antecedent to the park and bus stop benches. Did the tree always know its destiny would be to find itself carried on Christ's back? He queries:

> did you crawl
> from a swamp
>
> to rest at last
> on that man's back? (part III, 1-4)

The meaning of trees in Montoya's poetic world appears in a vertical plane as the upright jury of trees, which combines with horizontal wood *across* the collection, forming a motif of the Christian cross. The bus stop bench appears again in section 8 of "generation," playing a supportive role to all kinds of human drama:

> *you wept on an orange bench,*
> *the trees were not ashamed.*
> *the bench did not have a name*
> *but you baptized it anyway.*
> *was this the birth of stuttering? (19-23)*

The wooden cross that bore the weight of Jesus materially represents his jury, whereas, in a very mundane, late capitalist fashion, the wooden park bench provides the weary with respite but also a place to sit with their entangled unrest, a state like an affective condemnation put upon the racialized and gendered un- and underemployed. Montoya's trees are empowered to judge but also offer daily support for the underclass that struggles between a socially manufactured hell and the ever-present divine.

Natural elements become players in the speaker's cosmology, but Montoya does not propound his world vision. In contrast to Whitman's poetry, there is no suggestion that we should see the world as the speaker does, nor does he generalize his experience to the human universality of Neruda's poetry. In fact, the power of Montoya's poetry is not in the surprising glory of its humble subjects a la Mary Oliver and Luis Omar Salinas but rather in the constancy of his humility. Nor is Montoya's poetic I a special perceiver. He is simply aware, unlike others, that he is unremarkable yet divine. His philosophical and performative poetry unveils this unacknowledged fact, seeking to provide solace and empowerment for the multiply oppressed Latin@/x underclass of modern America.

Montoya builds this humility principally through two techniques: he stages the speaker's appearance relatively late in each poem, and when he does appear, he employs the first-person pronoun in lowercase ("i"). In most of Montoya's poems, the first stanzas situate the commingling of a person, an object, and a force of nature in an expansive physical environment where the poetic I takes his place (see "pákatelas," cited above). After assuming rather than asserting his role as a conscious perceiver of the world, the speaker then turns declarative, and an "i" emerges. The "i," perhaps inspired by e. e. cummings, exists along with poem titles also in lowercase, and because an "i" is not the same as a proper name, the "i" deemphasizes the particularity of the speaker. Like revering the flurry of stars in the night sky to suddenly focus on just one, the speaker imbues strength in the humble "i" through extensive use of the grammatical colon (:). The colon visually signals the reader to pause and pay closer attention to the spiritual quest of the "i," now among rather than amid a divine field. The "i" renders the speaker cosmically small while the colon punctuates his worthiness.

In essence, the colon is diegetic, guiding the reader from a celestial perspective to a distilled expression of self. Where the colon should indicate privileging self over the environment and its actors, we see sustained humility instead. Because Montoya's poetic world carefully allies mutual influence among dehierarchized elements and beings, the colon discerns the self in intimate relationship with its environment. The colon focalizes self in confluence with the disparate forces creating and receiving conditions in an animate field where the self is but one locus. Rather than set him apart, the structural introduction of the I later in Montoya's poems followed by the colon fortifies his connection with the energetic field he describes, rendering the speaker's luminous humility as one of the more distinguishing attributes of Montoya's poetry.

In Montoya's poetry, nature's inherent divinity contextualizes the nefarious as an expression of human frailty rather than as a condemnation of evil. All are among the anointed, including those in Montoya's *flor y canto* who, striving to vocalize, breathe, and sing, deliver the divine in a communal reflection. By bridging humanlike subjectivity into the animate and inanimate alike, the stuttering "i" breaks open the encasement of categories and liberates readers from dualistic thinking, breath and song erasing the boundary between what is considered living and what we qualify as dead. His philosophical premises are performative practices that soften the distinctions between these seeming opposites, honoring his dying body and the vibrancy of his soul. The poem "generation" is neither technically superior to Montoya's other poems nor thematically all-encompassing. Its vantage point, however, clearly introduces the central concerns of Montoya's oeuvre, his aesthetic approach, and his distinctive vision, creating a cogent orientation to appreciate *a jury of trees* as a whole.

Notes

[1] It must be noted that breath figures into the work of his mentor, Philip Levine, particularly powerful in his poem "After Leviticus" (*The Mercy Poems*, New York: Knopf, 1999), and later developed into the subject of *Breath: Poems* (New York: Knopf, 2004).

[2] From Nahautl, the language of the Aztecs, the expression "*In Xóchitl, In Cuícatl*" distinguishes the pre-Cortesian cultural practice where aurally

delivered poetry conveyed discourse of religious and philosophical importance in Aztec culture.

[3] Similar images occur less frequently but nevertheless play a significant role in Montoya's *the ice worker sings and other poems* (Tempe, AZ: Bilingual Press, 1999).

[4] For further analysis of the body and its role in subjectivity, see my forthcoming monograph *Shame Hurts: How the Soma Racializes in Latin@/x Literature.*

colón-ization

EARLY POEMS

. . . it was before everything came crashing down as if struck by a single stroke of lightning. before their boats brought them with their diseases, and their cannons, when they were still groping in the caves of europe trying to understand the meaning of fire and rock and wood.

the sun was laughing. an old man, an old woman worked the garden side by side. there was the smell of water and mud, a sweet taste that came with the breeze. there were children playing, their voices spilling over into song. the woman whispering prayers as she planted seeds. the man stroking the first blades of corn finding their way to the sun . . .

lorena's whisper

for lorena who died on the ninety nine, that drunk man hitting her head on, wrapping both behind their wheels

when i listen hard
i can almost hear the vines of birds
or just the leaves whispering
your name lightly on their tips, almost
laughing, as if they were trying to speak to me,
trying to remind me of that summer
when wasps surprised you while picking,
and you, looking as if you were crawling into the earth,
curled up like a baby
who's never been born. you almost died that day.

it scared your father,
the way you swelled up,
and he decided that the fields were no good
for you, you'd be educated.
i'd see you in the summer
with your books, your nice smelling clothes,
your father working extra jobs.
i knew you begged him
to let you work, ashamed of seeing
him slowly fail, his body bent
from the fields
and when you ditched
to defy the path he chose
he beat you until you returned.

still, you hung with gringos
from your classes, the college ones,
as if you grew up with them,

as if their parents and yours
knew the earth together.
did they understand your rough
stained hands?
at school when you walked by us
and one would mumble
'wanna be white girl,'
or 'bitch' or 'slut'
you'd look at me,
trying to ask me something,
i'd turn away, ashamed.
I knew you were mexicana

your father's language fresh
daily in your mouth

i was angry.
the summer before,
we were in a ditch, your skirt
sticking to your skin, your small breasts
showing through, i kissed
you, smelling of sulfur and perfume,
but you pulled away,
saying it wasn't right
for cousins to be this way.
i was angry at your strength, the way you never
told your father how I let them treat you,
the way you talked to me at home,
as if we were still kids
having dirt clod wars in the grape fields.

i remember the college party
in your senior year, the white one, your eyes ready
to take it all in, and you returned

with the eyes of our grandmother.
i remember the night in back of popsie's bar
drinking pisto, talking how they pulled a train
on you, each taking his turn with your brown flesh,
how fat louie said you deserved it,
that it never would've happened if you had stuck
with your own, that you were a puta anyway
and then my fist in his soft
face, feeling his nose explode
him falling to the ground and me kicking him
over and over
until skeeter and prax pulled me back,
fat louie lying there senseless.
how skeeter and prax
came with me to fresno's white side,
my '73 montigo, a tire iron in the back seat,
images of you and white men
in my eyes.

at your grave, the yard surrounded
by vines, the sun going down, the smell
of grapes drying on the trays sweet in the hot air, I sit

running my hands over the hot
metal letters of your name
waiting for wasps to whisper.

regeneration

he can hear them in the other room,
his mother scolding her daughter
'you have to give more money,
they're gonna shut off the power.'
'you know i ain't got no money,
i had to buy stuff for the baby.'
he checks the door again for the last time
and flips on the fan to drown out
his breathing. his chest is already
hurting, but he doesn't care,
it'll be over soon. he looks
into the bathroom mirror, past
his long hair, past the black-grey bags
under his eyes and concentrates
on the dark center of a single socket
that threatens to tell of a death
he's been dying for nineteen years.
he snaps his eyes shut.

He puts the pipe to his mouth, his lips
taking the glass like a lover's tongue
as he strikes the lighter and looks past
his tremendous nose along the thin line
of a blackened tube and finally
centers on the bowl-stuffed brillo pad.
from the bottom of his lungs he begins
to pull as he puts fire to the stone
and smell of a melted rock

flowers in the large holes of his nostrils.
he pulls and begins to lose his air
like a shotgun blast. it'll all be over soon,
his mother begging God to kill her
in the night, his sister rocking
the child to a melody of gunfire.
they all begin to fade, the cops
begging his spick ass to move,
the ragged clothes of his family,
the whirling puddle of Jesús's pooling
blood, and even his own cowardice,
him cowering before boys who beat
Jesús dead. everything begins
to fade in a haze of adrenalin

and it's over now, he can continue
he is a man again as he exhales
out the window the white smoke
                    of his life.

tenochititlan, 1523

. . . and it was true. they had found the
strange bird in texcoco while fishing, when the
sun was finally lowering itself to sleep. and
everyone wondered at the mirror in the
forehead of the unknown bird, if the visions it
kept playing over and over again were true;
the bearded men who rode great beasts,
throwing azteca babies onto the point of each
other's blades, laughing as if they had just
discovered a new game; the hairy men fucking
wildly, with vengeance, the mexica women;
the hunting of the men; the enslavement, the
chopped off hands, the skin of the dying
elders lying limp at their burnt feet . . .
and it was true, all of it was true, only the
stench of the men was like spoiled meat and
was heavier than imagined, and the pain
could never have been anticipated, the
surprise and shock lasting so long. they were
so evil. so greedy and nothing could satisfy
their desires, they had everything, and it was
not enough.

cucaracha

from the walls they come,
through cracks, like guerrillas,
attacking with precision.
no crumbs for these, only large
game will do.

stronger and smarter
they are, or perhaps just hungrier,
like millions of tiny
coyotes
coming to take from my plate
while i sit at the table.

tonight i will sit in the dark
and wait for them, feeling
first the tickle on my hands
and neck like a lover's
tongue, the rustling in my hair
like a summer's rain and
then the eyes will focus.
there will be an army cheering,
claiming victory

let's just kiss and say goodbye

going out to the mejía family.
in memory of práxedis

it happened that night when birds sang the song of the storm
and a little girl asked her mother the time,
when your cousin the football star
            gave florence a rose and told her,
'i love you, baby, let's go to the orchard and make it.'
when your mom was at home and your father drinking,
                        it happened
prax, you drove right through that center divider of the 99,
                        droopy eyed from kj
and smashed headlong into a car full of a family.
we're not gonna argue about it, it happened and you're dead.
i'm not going to say you were a great man,
or that you were beautiful, you had the face of a boar.
you were from calwa, son of a mechanic
and a woman with the strength of a sow.
you were the boy who wrestled God
in the back seat of a '73 montigo and went to city college
for five weeks in diesel engines,
who came to the big game with his box,
manhattans blaring in tune with his voice,
who held me when my chest was cut with a rose,
who called me brother, carnal.
prax mejía, i have come here for you,
to this dirty old 99, glass and blood gone, come to watch you
dance as i sing, cars passing again and again in blurs,
come to finally grieve, to plant your cross by the roadside,
i've come to kiss the lips of your memory.

love at the beginning

tonight for a moment as the owl sleeps
i'm going to dust this city's dirt from my clothes
the dry hot deaths that bring the strongest to their knees.
i'm going to run headlong through a rainstorm
dodging lightening blasts and hurdling rivers
as wolves howl on a peak of purple darkness.
with my nose flaring, the sulfur of the fields will not deter me,
i'm going to come through to a background of laughing cars
and screaming
                    sirens.
my forehead pushing forward to the street
of your house, i'm going to come with the smile of a boy,
my smile,
my hands offering callouses, offering struggle.
tonight as the owl sleeps, i'll come with the silence of a cricket,
with the intensity of a flower and for an instant, a second,
before i tell you it's starting and bring the guns,
feathers will flow from my mouth to tell you, mi amor, my soul,
a kiss before we pray. i gather the stars like berries
and bring them to light your face, let me again smell
the skin of your stomach,
let me wash your feet with my lips,
nibble the meat from behind your knees.

whispered fruit

THE POSTHUMOUS MANUSCRIPT

generation

1

i stutter.
the streets demand this:

the word stumbling forth
off the tongue

from the back of the mouth
from the throat
from the gut

from the lips
and onto the pavement
of my city.

i try to sing
to bring order to things
to bring rhythm to the theatre of rocks
and tears and potholes and dust

but the pavement requires a precise
sound, the correct vernacular
of witness. so i stutter

past alleys lit by flames
lashing up from a rusted can.

i stutter past churches
and children hanging onto the legs

of their mothers, at the apartments
which hold the memories
i left like bad apples.

i stutter and am embarrassed
because somehow
there is something
beautiful
in all of this.

2

tonight i am not a poet.

the stars are here.
my dog kuma sits alone
and an old flower falls
onto the moon.

this is an old sadness.
i ache at the sea. *what*
did you bring to us
sweet sister? come
let me add my measure
of salt to your white lips.

tonight i have nothing
to do with songs. instead
i speak to my legs
like old friends arriving
from the sea with words
in their pockets.

tonight i am not a poet.

i speak words forbidden:
hope love
beauty faith
soul spirit.

i speak to the trash
cans lining the road.
i say, "look up! look up!
thy redemption draws nigh!"

i watch
young lovers
stroll my street, stumbling
shyly into embrace.
they sing.
they breathe
like the trees
praising God.

3

as a boy i was taught
about technologies, messiahship
and about darwin's golden wink

but i never understood
the technology of love
losing its daughter on a dirt road

between peaches
and grapes, dust and air,
when the boy of twenty dreams
was murdered
for the sweet fruit
between his cousin's thighs:

i wept and still find
myself throwing down
tears for the twenty dreams
and the boy who held them
in a fistful of hope.

i wept for myself
and the ants who wailed
as if at the end of the world.

surely
the ants came
from their hills
of crushed fruit
bearing witness
to the crime
in poems like salt
that last an eternity
on the face.

this began my lessons
on the correct manner
of stuttering,

on the beauty
of truth as it mourns a city
lost in the morality of machines.

4

O, how i wish for the sea.
like a kiss.
the salty tear
of my boyhood
before trees
before fear
where even
the seagull
did not know my name.
the sea
and the glass.
a tender knee kneeling
into the surf
and a smile
a giggle,
the hair falling
limp with a wave
onto the smooth
forehead of innocence.
o, how i wish for the sea,
like a name
written
on white stone.

5

the city coughs.
my friends, noses to the stone
and tar of streets,
are afraid of clouds,
the way they part open

like a pink-brown mouth,
like the promise of salt
on the skin.

they are afraid of things eternal.
they are afraid of finding joy

in anything other than metal
and wheels and the imagination

of shoe venders.

here, in the city that coughs,
beauty is believed to be the fly
that, finally, lies dead.

beauty is the elimination
of cockroaches and the people
who have made treaties with them.

6

my sister is weeping
in the park
between the graffiti
and the bus stop.

a siren sounds
off to the east
and a lady
on the pay phone
laughs into the haze
of streetlamps and stars.

something's going on.

hell is doing an imitation
of a street corner
but only the people
in diamonds and suits
are convinced by the disguise.

something's going on.

my sister is weeping
between the corner
and the museum,
nestled in a locked stall
of the park's bathroom.

she keeps sobbing,
“God! God!”
it comes out of her mouth
like a stutter.

7

i stutter.
this is not like singing.
this is like penance.

i came marching
through the streets
looking for the child carrying
a leaf, for the wind and the trees
dancing against the progress of the city.

i came marching,
preaching the destruction
of all that is not science

placing the mountains
and rivers of my conscience

onto the altar of things dead.

this is all true.
the altar is on fifth street
between the dumpsters
and city hall.

there too you will find
the charred remains
of words still
trying to be spoken:

faith.
hope.
love.

i never expected resurrection.
i never expected blood.

and though i wanted nothing
but that which created itself,
that which crawled
from a swamp,
i dreamed.

and though i never wanted dreams,
i dreamed
of walls and words
wandering through my childhood:

east side locos

con/

safos

lion was here

the revolution will not be televised

i dreamed
of the hope i had
found in spray cans

and glue bags
and the desires
bubbling up from my
belief in nothing
and everything, myself.

though i never wanted anything
but that which created itself

i dreamed of a forehead
plowed with thorns,
and hands flowering blood
onto the sadness
of children,
blood blossoming
my scars into life.

and now my words
stumble out,
a bit crooked
and scared,
but testifying
to a jury of trees.

8

this, now, is how i pray:

what will erupt
from your whisper today?

you have spoken
into dance
the wild hair
of trees.

they crawled poemlike
from your breath.

what red fruit
will find itself
sweetly
spoken
into life?

where cain came
with his rock raised
against the forehead
of humanity

you wept on an orange bench.
the trees were not ashamed.
the bench did not have a name
but you baptized it anyway.
was this the birth of stuttering?

what hope will you whisper
today into the heart of the city?

breathe, o God
o Christ

breathe your tree's fruit,
red, riverlike
into these streets,
desperate,
like a lonely cheek.

9

i come from the battlefield
of concrete and bricks.
leonard is my dead.
eddie and prax
people the wall of my sorrow.

i come from the shadows
in a city baking under the sun.
a dead boy is circled by ants
and my memory is shocked at itself.

here, in my city, they say
"peace and safety!"
they say there is no war here

but since '73
i've been running for my life
rat-tatting angelic machine guns

and hiding in shadows
with others like me,
scarred and eyeballing everything.

the names of my generation
are three unspeakable syllables
stuttering onto the breast of this world.

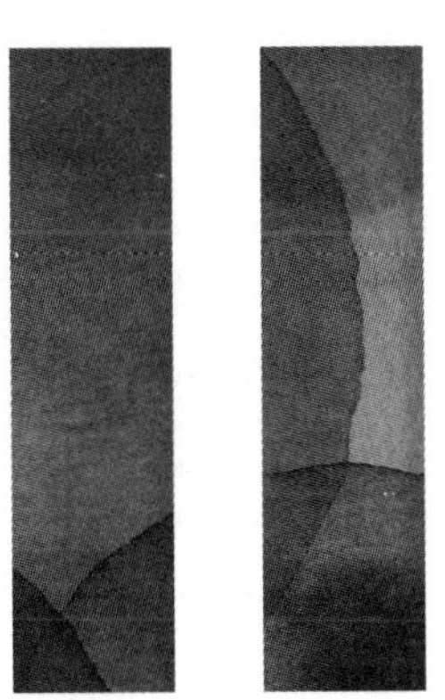

song fruit

simple songs
crawl
from the day's
mouth:

the bird
in mid-
flight

the honey
of a woman's
breath

the taco vender
reciting
darío
in a moment
of passion.

i am learning
arias
in my back-
yard.

my dog,
kuma,
is bewildered.

and

the day blushes

happily

from

its split lip.

song lesson

para kb

they say
this is poetry

the way water falls
from rocks to pools
of purple algae,

the glare of the trees' red bark
demanding my hand,
          skin upon skin,

                    and

plants pushing up
          demanding the face
                    of the sun
          as if for the first time.

sister
  it is
the breath
of Christ
teaching us
          to sing.

buscando

i am looking again.

the street's square jaw
        challenges
                the afternoon.
the rain
runs.

children
        play
        dice down
        the pitted paths
        of boarded up alleys.

i am looking for a man
        with hands
        wounded
        in the old fashioned way,
        without fanfare,
        without applause,
        but with moans

        —there will be birds
        picking food
        from a trash heap
        when i find him,
        a prostitute will be hiding
        her face behind a mask
        of powder. relief

will come with a word
kissing the cheek of a child—

the black smoke
of a burning house
on the city's south side
dances madly
into the heavy gray
of evening.

i am looking
and sky water is cool.

three thousand lost kisses

the night swoons
    to the hip-hop
    of gunshots
    and stars.

a young woman's teeth
    challenge
    everything

about sorrow's suitcase
of explanations

and i am learning to hope
    like a bird
    learns
    its first
    affair
    with wind
    and sun

    like an orange
    learns
    to take flight
    into the mouth
    of a boy
    in summer.

the trees are prophesying.
the mountains are waiting
for the long trek to the sea

and the sea
        waits
        like a lover
anticipating the kiss
        of three thousand
        lost kisses.

the night swoons
        and the trees
        begin their blue-black
        dance
in the wind.

crush

slowly,

as if
to taste
the red mud,

the blossomed trees
softly lean.

the birds
are having
their discussions:

—spring

—the avalanche
of sorrows
settling
at last
their ground

—and lovers
arriving in the park.

it isn't sadness

that brings
me here:

the bench
weathered
with scars
and peeling paint;

the grass gray
with exhaustion.

i come to study bones of hope:
someone has etched a crucifix
into the cracked skin of a tree.

the flowers
don't know
it's too soon
for their smiles,

that rain
still has a day
to thunder
along to its place,

the white sigh
of night
still desires
its
say.

the petal-cups
open

as if
to the first hint
of a kiss

and i am singing

as if
with the first
bruised
mouth.

tuesday night

the night stumbles
its way through the streets
trying to hide
from stars
which wheeze
in and out of alleys
like an old man
finds his dreams
        appearing and disappearing
        throughout the long memory
        of his life.

i haven't yet written a poem
        but i keep
        searching

like a boy who has lost his legs
        somewhere
        in a city
        that has
        only one mile left
        to see.

i know life has to be here somewhere.
        i keep believing.
        i am the child strolling the streets
        with his father in 1972
        trying to understand the leather

of work wrapping his hands.
this is the birth of hope.

the night is a beggar: his pockets full of promise.
i go to sleep.
tomorrow
the sun will come
with its trumpet
delivering us all
from the obnoxiousness
of stars.

declaration

i have found
the face
of story
lying again.

i'm tired.

i'm a moth
on sunday.

i'm rain
looking
for a cup's
crippled rim.

this is my decision:
blindfolded
i will look for truth
in the rough skin
of wood
sticking up
at the sky
from the largest hill
at the dump,

in the sound
of a car
on its way
to church,

in the smell
of beans
boiling away
into the night.

criminals

. . . and the poets gathered
    under the gossamer wind
        of their words.

the silence of war
    found its lawyer
    in our hearts.

some erected
    monuments
    to the beauty of despair
    as it descends the huge
    staircase of existence.

    —but the bombs were exploding
    around us like political campaigns
    full of smiles and careful words—

others
began to give
oaths
to their legs
        and the lopped off
        tips of their noses.

others worshipped the calloused hand
    of metal
    from martini glasses and mansions.

—but war waged
and we all just wanted
to whistle our tunes
about the power
of a carefully powdered cheek
or the weight of the world
as we gave interpretation
of the earth's first breath.
but all around us
the bullets became sharp—

none of us wanted to die
— no matter how much we tried to convince you—
but our poems
returned
with white canes
to beat us
to death
for our silence.

spanish vernacular

the stars
tonight
smile
sadness

and
a woman
walks
alone on the streets
mumbling secrets
about
bricks
and poverty.

of course,
omar is lecturing
the yerbas
and nopales
about the giddy giggle
of despair

and

i am left
to figure
out splinters
and their long coats
of blood.

miguel is still dead
but some-

how
i know
an onion
protested
the executioner's
buckteeth.

some- how
the stars are talking
about hopes and clouds.

eschatology

a boy finds
    the night
    and himself
    waiting

    like the world waits
    and the trees
    and the mountains
    and the rivers wait
    and the seas wait
    like everything waits

the boy finds
    the stars
    like his toes
    anticipating
    a sky full
    of jazz
    and clouds

constellation

there are the stars
and the sickle stare
of the moon

there are the frogs
dancing in the joy
of the ditch and the crickets
serenading everything

there are the trees
and the huge shadow
of the wind whispering
the old hymns of my childhood

and of course, there are the stars again.
winking at me like a curious woman.

i am learning to breathe.

tree

did you crawl
        from a swamp

        to rest at last
on that man's back?

or did you have purpose
        even

        in the mouth
        of the poet

weeping on a tuesday
in the afternoon

        as the sun was beginning
        its long walk
        to the sea?

or perhaps you were born
from the skin
        of that man

        learning at the first
the way flesh parts

to allow the body's
sap to flow

onto a world wounded
by its own hand.

did you begin,
too,
to weep?

did you hate
the men
who did this thing?
who showed angels and demons
the way we paint
the canvas of history?
or did you say,
“bow! bow!
and receive your kingdom
of meat!?”

i tell you
i am only a boy.
i, too, moan
with you

as the body of wind enters
like a stone
opening its mystery.
this is how one finds his knees.

tell me
what did it feel
like to understand first
the mystery of a veil
torn in two?

what swamp
        did you crawl from

        to rest at last
                on the back
                of that broken man?

        or

        were you born
        on the highest hill
        of the dump
        shaped like a skull?

ojo

i want to catch you
          dark fruit.

          dagger.

give me your sweet salt.
          fall
                    into my shirt
                                        pocket

and i will carry you
          —bruised grape—

          until we exist
                    all alone.

forehead

i am not afraid
to be a romantic.

so i will say

"it is the mystery
of lines
that has shocked me."

—a smile
a frown
a sulking
scream
etching its
palm
print

onto your
great wall
of song—

the sudden
scar running
down
your side
is a valley

hoping
to produce
a symphony of sighs.

if you had to exist all alone
you would fall
to the ground:

but the eyebrows
have always wept
at your feet.

sombra

i speak to you shadow
as i would
speak to clouds:

you exist
in a moment
of hair

cascading over
a beautiful
neck.

you are my sorrow
or joy:

a rat in the trees,
a robin striking a pose.

i speak to you shadow
as i speak
to my own words:

you exist in a hollow
of hair

counted and catalogued

by a graceful mouth.

tiempo

where are you going?

you have never learned
to be eternal.

so put on your top hat
and stroll
into the libraries

whistling
round and round
the books of the gagged.

you assassin of silence,

you are a bull running in circles
singing towards
the revelation of everything.

ombligo

you are the pharisee
        of flesh.

when the ankle
        became crooked
                against
        the chin,

you began taking notes.

you hoard stories
        in your huge hole
                of accusations.

you claim
        the right
        to sentence
                the heart
                        for bleeding sourly
        onto your tongue.
        but your mouth is appleless.

i tell you,
no more cockroaches
will attend your recitations.
your breath is not sweet like truth.
the forearm will no
        longer
                weep

at the lies
you have swallowed.

your only hope is a man
calling himself
tortilla.

so,
come,
be slaughtered
in a garden of nopales.

be born, at last.

pierna

who conceived your craters
        or
        the slender
        bend of your knee?

what are the grape vines
        —winding their way

                under your skin—

attempting to say?

i tell you

        do not try to mask
                the torn lip
                        of the knee:

                                it is the crucial note
        in the song
                stinging the lies of madness.

if you tried to unmask your beauty
        you would die from frustration.

                tell me

        who created the joyful cry of this canyon?

toes

the toes too demand
the orchestra of light.

they are rising up
from the mud,
slogans slicing
up from their painted
position
at the nails.

they are tired
of
the faltering staccato
of fingers
drumming upon
the surface
of things

the toes can only dream about.

they are tired
of the language
of lips and tongues

discovering
the phenomena
of wind and breath and brick
—sounds echoing off

everything
as if accusing the toes
of their lonely

country
caught between
grass and dirt
and the blue blue

nostalgia
of sky.

they are demanding
respect
for the poetry
of balance,
for the beauty
of space
between two thighs

or between
heel and toe

as one finds
the surprise
of a forest

in its lovely sapphire
of stone and pine.

the toes rise up
demanding

to be seen
for the character
of the callous

or the cracked skin's
wonderful
sorrow
explained
in cryptography.

the toes, too, demand
the light's sullen surrender.

face

i am waiting
to understand
the poverty
of your cheek.

the salamander
          swallowing the long
          cinnamon look
of your eyes.

sea poem #1

the white lips
of the sea
are speaking:

they say
you are beautiful

a face full
of shiny stones

and clouds
that gather into the huge sky
of your breast.

pákatelas

1

this is a coyote's
song—
my song,

the confused guitar
wearing the banjo's mask

on the third
corner
of my dreams,

my eyelids escaping

over pyramids
and mountains,
in boats
over oceans and clouds:

my father's cheek
always speaks tewa

and his eyes are singing
from five
hills in durango.

but his tongue
has amnesia.

his songs
are gathered
from
neither
english thighbones
nor
spanish marrow

but from somewhere
in between.

¿pero dónde?

él dijo
—me vine desde allá
and i found myself
enredado
con cercos de alambre,
don't they know
que mi madre
es la tierra?—

and i must be his
son.
my eyes are
not quite
bastards

but homeless

in tierra
that, perhaps,

once
was
called
aztlán
or not.

but i
too
am from
in between.

"everywhere
and
nowhere"
tattooed below
my belly's
apex.

there are no spaces

between borders
and it is in the spaceless
that i find my lips

shuddering
people

césar
rubén
cuauhtemoc
gabriela
llorona
tiny y smokey
shy girl and monstro and chuy and boobi.

i find myself
in song
assaulting
the streets,

singing,
“i am large
i contain
multitudes,”

as if i was
busting out
cumbia style,
“pákatelas
pákatelas
pákatelas
da da da-ran”
with a line i saw scrawled
on a wall in pinedale.

but this is the question
always calling up
from the angry craters
of *calles*,

—as if it mattered, *this birth of breath into word—*

when was it that poems came crawling

from the lonely
recesses of my
gut?

was it the sea salt
kiss
of the sky
that became
my
muse?

or

was it
the murals of madness
whispering,
running out
from the stiff brush
of my father's mind
onto the walls
of the free clinics
in east
oak town?

This is all i know:

i came patiently behind
devouring the poverty
of my mother's spoon,

waiting

for my father
to
return
from the sea,

ringlets dangling from his nose
in the latest
revolutionary
fashion,
a silver faced
che
or
zapata,
pecked with beautiful slogans
like wind.

i came patiently behind
running as fast as I could
from the phantom of hair

and tongueless feet
that kept
threatening
from the
left

and
i found myself in the forest
speaking to pigs
whose squeals opened to the sky
like a peach
opens
its
anguish

to the wild starvation
    of ants.

was this the first poem?

the vernacular
of flying
    and crawling things?

we found ourselves
    —my family and i—

        in slow sludge
            groaning
                with our ojos covered
    by the peels of green mangos,

    kneeling by a cross
        crippled
    by a preacher's glass eye.

there, undaunted, in the land of the mutes
    my grandmother
    placed her hands
            into
    clouds
like masa

    begging breath
        from
    a pierced foot.

    still, the shattered
        elbow

of night

kept calling
with its
subtle teeth
of despair.
we hid in the trees
finding
the first roaches
laughing
like
sasquatch.

there I was schooled in the academy
of mud and fear.
there i learned the honeyed face
of sobs
babbling like brooks.

but when was it
that poetry pounded
itself
from between my lips
my sorrow
my hate,
past the club foot of my soul
and my toltec eyebrow?
it must have been
at the first church
that poetry wiggled
its way up my throat.

it began
at five,

at exactly five years,
        at exactly five in the afternoon,
under the pines
            next

to the house of hogs
                where i had discussed
        the riddle
                of dove work.

the petrified
        sequoia
        behind the red house
        became my brother's
        pulpit
        and i ushered

                our neighborhood
                        friends
        to rug samples
                set up
                        as legless pews.

my brother preached Jesus
        and how only he
                 could save us

                 from the soured breath
                           of sasquatch
        and the cockroaches
        who had hoisted
        our lives onto their backs.
we all knew

the olive garden
of night,

how the beekeeper's boy

found footprints
burrowed

into mud and needles
outside his wild window

prints bigger than the beekeeper's boots.

at the first church
us kids
shouted amens
and hallelujahs
to the jammin'
groove of grace
that bounced out
from my brother's
beautiful mouth

and
i would clap
and shake my legs
in rhythm
to tunes
only i heard.

there i began to notice
words,
like zacatecas
and seraphim,

like kentucky
and jericho
echoing
off the cheek
of everything
into song.

there, at the first church,
poetry began.

2

this is a coyote's

song

my song

stinging
the soft underbelly
of lies.

i breathe.
my eyes blink
boldly.

this is not
insanity's tight skirt,
the maniac's love song.

my throat vibrates
from boats
and land.

sometimes i
sing

with my spanish
eyebrow,

but always
    my tewa nostrils
        demand to know
            the meaning of song
                and flor
                    y
                    canto,

    demand to know
        the genesis

            of things:

        once, i was standing
        in clouds
        liking

    the concrete of
    my life.

    i found birds whistling

    from the south

    corner of a heart.

    and the songs
    could be heard
    bouncing

PÁKATELAS

    off the brick walls
    of chinatown.

i've been here
in this maze
ever since.
all the trees are gone
and i'm left wondering

how was it
that we came here?

on boats?
trains?
horses?
in cars, hoopties
on highway five
or sixty-six?

i think—and this has to be the truth
there are no other
explanations—

the streets
slowly goose stepped
onto the scene.

the wild hairs
of power lines
and phone lines
lip
the sky
like schizoid
orders,

others barking up
from the farmer's chest,

a huge beautiful chest
covered with
banana breath
and leaves

and, you know, there is the laughter
of muñecos

menacing radio park,

a mother masking
her smile

to scold
a funny
boy
bounding around

like a tiger.

radio park
clinton
first
alabama
muskogee

streets
styling
'round the park
'round the junkies
pink bathroom
that neighbor's
POETS ASSOCIATION ART GALLERY:

(this is how i learned about the armed propaganda
of words bombing the streets)
"o, distinguished colleagues of the rhythmic rhyme of images,
i wrote this poem about the battle for our integrity
after teaching my class on the most holy universality
of Shakespeare and the Whitman rhythm of the self
please . . . bow your heads:

o, poetry
save us
with your iconoclastic
wall of faces.

o, poetry
of the holy hooded
order, deliver us
from the evil
of code switchers
and the bad poetry
of the nezahualcoyotl
types who don't
belong here anyway."

this is when my sister
starts scattin'
on the corner
of the world.

she explains
everything
with the be-bop
bounce of the hip-hopsters,
bubblegum

and nines
blasting
through the air.

¿entiendes, méndez?
here, let me give it up,

the whole canela stick,
the secrets of horchata
order:
there were no theories
to explain the poverty
of leno lópez's limp.

and the cops never
found the cockroaches
that stole his hope

on the afternoon
that he learned
to carry his eyes

in pockets
that don't stain
with pain.

i'm tired of photos
so when leno leapt
into the final
sigh
and discovered himself

swinging
from shoelaces and fear

i left my camera at home

listen, o beautiful
reader
the
streets
slowly stomped
onto
the scene.

this is how it must have happened:

corner by corner
i fell in love.
pound's mural

of the wet
black
boughs
on the sixth street wall.

but still
my tongue coiled
slowly around
the sad slouch of his justice.

still i carried neruda
in my back pocket
like a grip of coins.

on eighth street *—i never knew, carnal. they never*

williams displayed

his pieces
in a glass gallery

told us of your
spanish tongue
of the rolling r's

and i wept
for the beauty
of green shards
and wheelbarrows

on tenth street
i was astonished to see
suits pushing shakespeare
in needles to schools

guillermo, i love you
you have wonderful
bold breath
but they've dressed
you up
in a miniskirt and
heels
and put you on the
corner
of their alabaster
politics.

i want to change your name
to billy bad boy
dress you in creased
dickies and winos
and teach you the language
of my tío loco's
pachuco priesthood—

they were beautiful,

but always
they existed on top
        or below
on avenues and highways,
                and i stuttered
at the
                opera
of their exhaust-
                ing lines.

i like salsa
        and salt.

so i found my way to the side streets
        of the barrio,
        where Miguel
                still sliced
                onions
                and was respected
                for it.

where el maestro valley joe
still called out his spanish
        volunteers.
there i found i could discuss
        the lines

there i understood
the rhythmic rings
        of my slaughtered ear
        drums.

i knew all about the cop's wrought iron hand of justice
and the pale poverty of the child's tongue

murdered in the officialdom of lies.

i only wanted to understand
hope
as if hope was saying,

"hoy sufro sola-
mente."

i wanted to understand the madness
of my own divided

cheeks.

so I began to make up my songs.

the sun comes
making its declarations
of light
while shadows,
cheekless
shyly make their stand.

the busted eye of a green olds winks by
and a little boy
imagines God,
universe breath and all,
considering onionlike
street curbs
lullabying children.

i sang,

here they came

with their draculian
thirst
and murdered
the moon
with conquest.

i wanted to understand the peacock
feather
of truth

here. vato. here.

the streets slowly stay the same.

i look at my mother's knee

and realize
someone
has stolen
her shakespearean
saunter.

(the irish too must have wept at the famished potato of his soul)

i consider my father's

beautiful face,

and his eyes conveniently seem to sing
"o, poetry
of norte américa
you are the syphilitic
whore
beautiful
on belmont avenue

only
when the sun
and moon
have conspired

to leave us
in streetlamps of darkness.

you pretend
to be healthy

as if
your teeth
were not chipped
and crawling
with the black hole
of lies
waiting
to suck
up
the truth.
you recite
the vallejos and nerudas and daríos
hikmets and castillos

while
assassinating their
lips

on the faces of shy children.

you betray the word
with a kiss.

o, poetry
of norte américa

tú escribes libros
de las maneras
de amar,
o, imperialismo dulce—

while spreading your legs
for the cucarachas."

i consider your face, too
poetry
and discover it a bit sacred
and beautiful.

i consider you
norte américa
and i am wounded.

i love to sing
but
am

frightened
by your regional
teeth.

américa
i sing
américa.

i sing you
water and rock
earth and sky,
américa.
i sing, *américa.*

américa, i sing . . .

leukemia poems

FROM A POET'S DEATH JOURNAL

i am barely thirty
but already death came
three times:

once in khakis and
shiny shoes
with a carload of sickle-
shaped stares

once in fire
that didn't burn
as if i was a bush

and once flowing
from a long tongue
of lies

i am not afraid

o peach,
            open your meat

and together we'll be a song.

peach, be soft and weep gently

sweetly
over the valleys of my tongue

your red-brown heart is a song

your skin is bitter like suffering

and your breath
soft and orange

like a child dancing

giggling at the wonderful
stomp of his feet.

this is the first death

before leukemia
before nurses
before cortez and colón
and boats
and royal decrees
before a river and a monk:

tears ripped from behind my eyelids

this is about death
about the skin's way of wrinkling
a young man.

this is about slaughter
about pigs finding
their pit and a man
with a knife in his hand

mariachis moan
into the evening
and children are laughing,
running around the chairs of the old,
old ways.

same old story like
the one i already have
tattooed scarlike
onto the brown
leg of my soul

this is about boats,
and the day of coming
faces drawn back
like old men

about pockets,
about backs
looking for their shirts

this about dreams
and their way of being forgotten.

this is the scars of a man's hand
his feet and forehead,
water and blood.

the rose:

a song weeping
in the house of her father

the hips:

a declaration of praise

her eyes:

almonds
wounding my heart.

once i was a flower.
my sister was too
in the rows and rows
of streets and buildings
held up by bricks,
concrete and fear

we found fragrance in dance
and song

i understand the language
of birds

i was a flower

a chrysanthemum
something purple
or bloody and proud

once i was a bunch of yellow-
white petals

i was, on a walk south
on fruitdale ave,
a whistle waiting
for the next breath.

i do not desire mirrors
i do not desire
the old pattern
of my hands
                    or,

trees peopling the paths
of my barrio.

show me the blue veins
running out from your hope
into streets mountains and rivers
blue and white with laughter

and i will discover at last
a new
sonata of creation
a new song

vibrating from the throat
of God.

come and gather
my eyeballs
like fruit
from a tree
and see
the other cheek of the world.

when i came into the city
of this world
i was already
an old man
with yellow teeth
beginning to litter
my history

i knew nothing about
conquest
but my cheeks
understood everything
as if an ancestor
had hidden himself
beneath my skin.

the day is lonely
and full of people
we're all hungry

today i forget what poetry
is supposed to do.

i have nothing left
to retreat to.

there are no more machines
to keep me busy
to keep my mind
mumbling along
into space
          and space
          and space

          and space

the poor are weeping
in the gallery
of insane cameras
and microphones

i was born in this town
with words under my tongue

in this town of television
screens tattooing us

until what we see
isn't real

people keep telling
me to paint the
face of this town
with my tongue

but image is a whore

and all i can do

is stutter

as a child
            i was a flower
                        dancing for my pueblo.

this was long ago
            when *siete lenguas*
            was a cumbia

i have never seen tigers
so still.

they remind me of love.

do you sweat, God?
are tears enough?
do you bleed, God?
do you bleed?
yes. yes.
night and sweat.

the moon is finding
its light in your eyes
and your lips
are two birds
whistling
into the sky
of my breast.

is that the glory
of Christ
resting on your forehead?
be silent
so that i will know
we're living.

i will close my eyes
and smell the whisper
of your shadow.

i do not understand
the way an eye
or a smile

wounds
like a rose

with its breath
on a warm
night.

i am not afraid to be wounded by you, sweet singing birds.

i am afraid only of the lukewarm silence
slicing the ear drum.

i see too many writers afraid of their vision,
afraid to admit their hope

* * *

i desire high places
roofs of buildings
tops of stairs
to sit in the clouds
and breathe

to hear the city
laid out:
          a slow, sad
                    song.

* * *

o God teach
    me
    the tongue
                    of joy

* * *

a guitar wanders
through the streets
of the city

and one day God fell in love.
it was the kind of love
that starts just above
the gut, but below the heart
and aches and touches things
and is not ashamed
or afraid
to be a fool,

and God, who one day fell in love,
began to dance
over his love
like a silly kid
at the beach
in the sand with the waves
roaring a wonderful beat

and on the day God fell in love
He came below
the hospital window

with mariachis
who strummed their
guitars

he sang,
o, my love, my love,
your smile and eyes a poem
striking my cheeks

i am blushing
i am a child giggling

and God sang
you are beautiful to me
in your hair
are the oceans.

one of your eyes is the moon
the other contains the stars

little bird,
where have you been hiding?

the clouds were lonely
for your song today.

the sun got lost
on its way to the sea.

and i was left to study
the poisoned blood in my heart.

little bird,
where are the feathers
of your voice?

didn't you know
that i am a tree
a bit crooked

my trunk scarred
but i stand

i am waiting for you

come, let us find
the canal's cold kiss,

honey's sting
                    to the tongue.

one day i asked God to stamp eternity on my eyes. i didn't know what i was saying. i only knew that i wanted to understand cheekbones and the hope of clouds.

i have no flowers.
i have no diamonds.

o God
            my God!
                        o God

my tongue limps
into the evenings
in search of eyes

something behind my eyes
wants to leap
into this evening
of peach meat,

the language of water and salt
but sweet, sweet
like the death of a grape

i'm cold and this night is not cruel
but i want to stand up
and accuse the stars

Your name is like a sea
that swallows time,

a tongue splitting
open
the belly of clouds
with its whispered fruit

ABOUT THE AUTHOR

Andrés Montoya received his BA degree from California State University, Fresno, where he studied with Philip Levine and Corrinne Clegg Hales and cofounded the Chicano Writers and Artists Association with fellow student Daniel Chacón. He went on to earn his MFA degree from the Creative Writing Program at the University of Oregon, which was then directed by Garrett Hongo. Montoya published widely in such journals as *The Santa Clara Review, in the grove, Bilingual Review/ Revista Bilingüe,* and *Flies, Cockroaches, and Poets.* His first book, *the iceworker sings and other poems* (Bilingual Press, 1999), was awarded the 1997 Chicano/Latino Literary Prize from the University of California, Irvine. The published collection later won a Before Columbus Foundation American Book Award in 2000.

Born on May 18th, 1968, Andrés Montoya died from leukemia on May 26th, 1999, at the age of 31. After his untimely death, the Andrés Montoya Poetry Prize was created by Letras Latinas, the literary initiative of the Institute for Latino Studies at the University of Notre Dame to honor Montoya and his work. The prize is awarded to a first book by a Latino/a poet residing in the United States and includes a cash prize and publication by the University of Notre Dame Press.

photo: Francisco Domínguez

Additional biographical information can be found in Daniel Chacón's foreword, which is a moving tribute to the poet. In addition, Stephanie Fetta's introduction provides a scholarly analysis of Montoya's work.